Hal Leonard Student Piano Library

Piano Techniqu[e]

Book 2

Authors
Barbara Kreader, Fred Kern, Phillip Keveren, Mona Rejino

Director, Educational Keyboard Publications
Margaret Otwell

Editor
Carol Klose

Illustrator
Fred Bell

Book: ISBN 0-634-00427-1
Book/CD: ISBN 0-634-08975-7

HAL•LEONARD®
CORPORATION
7777 W. BLUEMOUND RD. P.O. BOX 13819 MILWAUKEE, WI 53213

Visit Hal Leonard Online at
www.halleonard.com

Dear Teacher,

Piano Technique Book 2 presents a *Warm-Up* and an *Etude* for each new technical skill students will encounter in **Piano Lessons Book 2**.

We suggest that you demonstrate each *Warm-Up*. Teaching by demonstration allows students to focus on the purely physical aspects of learning a new skill, such as hand and body position, or arm and finger movement. This helps them understand the connection between the movement they make and the sound they create.

Once students have learned the physical skill presented in each *Warm-Up*, they can use it to play the corresponding *Etude* with expression.

The *Musical Fitness Plan* on each warm-up page teaches new technical concepts and provides a check list for technical readiness:

- **Body and Hand Position**
- **Beautiful Tone**
- **Attention to Silence**
- **Dynamics**
- **Detached Tones**
- **Connected Tones**
- **Playing Hands Together**

By the end of **Piano Technique Book 2**, students will be able to produce a full-sounding tone with every finger and will be ready to play *staccato, legato,* and hands together, using a variety of different finger combinations. Having mastered these skills, students will have the confidence to move on to the technical challenges presented in **Piano Lessons Book 3**.

Best wishes,

Barbara Kreader   Fred Kern

Phillip Keveren   Mona Rejino

Dear Students,

You need an exercise plan to stay physically fit.

Like participating in sports, playing the piano is a physical activity that uses your whole body. **Piano Technique Book 2** will outline the *Musical Fitness Plan* you need to develop new musical skills.

Your *Musical Fitness Plan* includes:
- **Warm-Ups** – drills to develop new musical skills
- **Etudes** – music to practice using the new skills you learned in the *Warm-Ups*

It feels good to play the piano! Your teacher will show you how to play each *Warm-Up*. Follow the *Musical Fitness Plan*, paying careful attention to the way you use your body, arms, and fingers to create music. When you play, notice how the movement you make affects the sound you create. Once you have learned each *Warm-Up*, read and practice the matching *Etude*.

You are now ready to begin.

Have fun!

Barbara Kreader   Fred Kern   Phillip Keveren   Mona Rejino

Piano Technique
Book 2

CONTENTS

* Students can check activities as they complete them.

Musical Fitness Review

Use the following checklist to demonstrate the skills you learned in **Book 1**.

☐ **Sitting at the Piano**

Ask yourself:

- Am I sitting tall but staying relaxed?
- Are my wrists and elbows level with the keys of the piano?

☐ **Hand Position**

1. Let your arms and hands hang naturally at your sides. Notice the curve of your fingers.

2. Keep this position as you place your fingers on the keys.

   When you are playing the piano, keep your fingers in this curved position.

3. When playing with your thumb, let it rest naturally on its outside tip.

☐ **Beautiful Tone**
Place the weight of your whole arm behind each finger as you play.
Let your arm follow your fingers and listen for an even sound on each note.

☐ **Attention to Silence**
Release your arm weight during each rest, keeping your fingers on the keys.

☐ **Playing** *Forte*
Press the key to the bottom of the key bed with full arm weight.

☐ **Playing** *Piano*
Press the key to the bottom of the key bed with less arm weight.

☐ **Detached Tones**
Release the key as soon as you play it, letting your wrist bounce lightly.
Notice how your finger naturally rebounds and comes to rest on the key.

☐ **Connected Tones**
Pass the sound smoothly from finger to finger or hand to hand.

Take Another Look
Review Etude

Using all the confidence you gained in **Piano Technique Book 1**, celebrate your new musical skills! Play each finger with equal weight by letting your arm follow your fingers.

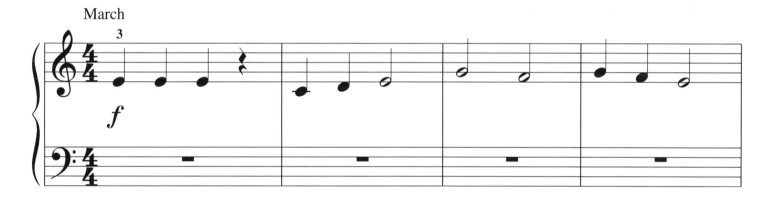

Accompaniment (Student plays one octave higher than written.)

5

Use with Lesson Book 2, pg. 4

Musical Fitness Plan

Use this checklist to review fitness skills and to focus on learning new ones.

Hand Position

Raise your hand and wave to your teacher with your fingers. Notice how your fingers move from the knuckles (*bridge*). As you press each key, play from the *bridge* of the hand with each finger.

Let your thumb rest naturally on its outside tip.

☐ **Beautiful Tone**
Place the weight of your whole arm behind each finger as you play. Let your arm follow your fingers and listen for an even sound on each note.

☐ **Playing *Mezzo Forte***
Press the key to the bottom of the key bed with medium arm weight. Listen to the sound you create.

☐ **Playing *Mezzo Piano***
Press the key to the bottom of the key bed with slightly less arm weight. Listen to the sound you create.

☐ **Connected Tones**
Pass the sound smoothly from finger to finger or hand to hand.

Playing Hands Together

When hands move in the opposite direction (*contrary*), let your arms follow your fingers.

To the Teacher: Demonstrate these warm-ups first. This will allow students to focus on the purely physical aspects of learning a new skill. Encourage students to play each warm-up in different octaves.

Warm-Ups

Rope Bridge *pg. 8*

When you walk across a rope bridge, you keep your body balanced behind each foot so you won't fall.

Let your arm follow your fingers as you walk them up and down the keyboard. Place the weight of your arm securely behind each finger as you play. Listen for an even sound on each note.

See-Saw *pg. 9*

A see-saw moves easily from one side to the other because it is balanced in the center.

Let the third finger of each hand act as the center of the see-saw. When you pass the sound from note to note, feel your arm weight shift from finger to finger. Watch your wrist move gently, like the ends of a see-saw, from side to side.

Rope Bridge

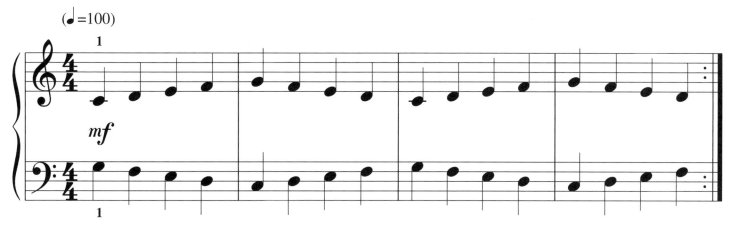

See-Saw

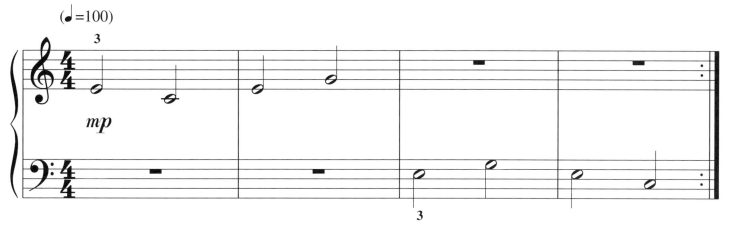

Rope Bridge

Accompaniment (Student plays one octave higher than written.)

See-Saw

Gently swaying

mp

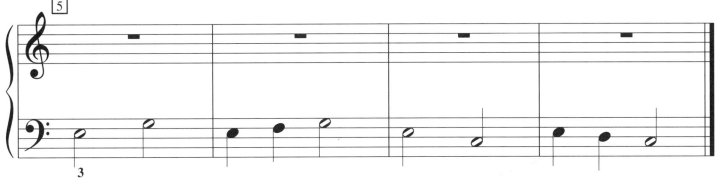

Accompaniment (Student plays two octaves higher than written.) 7/8 5

Gently swaying (♩=120)

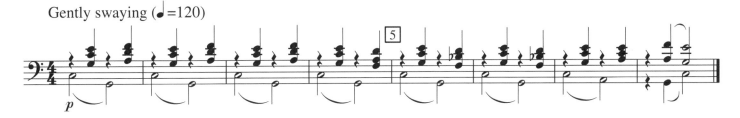

p

9

Use with Lesson Book 2, pgs. 6-7

Musical Fitness Plan

Use this checklist to review fitness skills and to focus on learning new ones.

☐ **Hand Position**

☐ **Beautiful Tone**

☐ **Attention to Silence**
Release your arm weight during each rest, keeping your fingers on the keys.

☐ **Playing** *Mezzo Forte*

 NEW!

Connected Tones – *Legato*
Pass the sound smoothly from finger to finger. Begin each phrase with a downward motion of the arm and end the phrase with an upward motion of the wrist.

NEW!

Detached Tones – *Staccato*
Release the key as soon as you play it, letting your wrist bounce lightly. Notice how your finger naturally rebounds and comes to rest on the key.

NEW!

Playing Hands Together
When hands move in the same direction (*parallel*), let your arms follow your fingers.

Warm-Ups

Red Light, Green Light *pg. 12*

9

In the game "Red Light, Green Light," you must be prepared to move and pause. In this warm-up, your fingers perform similar movements.

Your arm, hand, wrist, and fingers work together. Begin each phrase with a downward motion of the arm and end the phrase with an upward motion of the wrist.

Bee Cha-cha *pg. 13*

10

When you say "Cha-cha-cha!" it sounds like "short-short-long."

Let go of each staccato interval as soon as you play it. Let your wrist bounce gently on each quarter note and hold the half note.

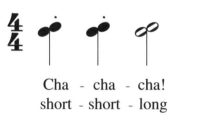

Cha - cha - cha!
short - short - long

10

Red Light, Green Light

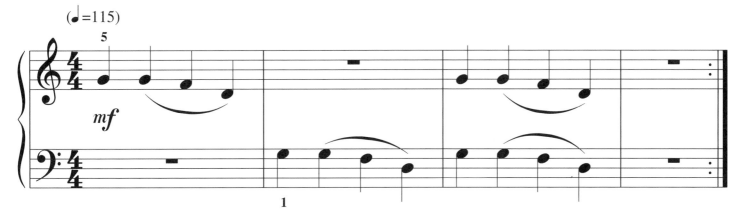

Bee Cha-Cha

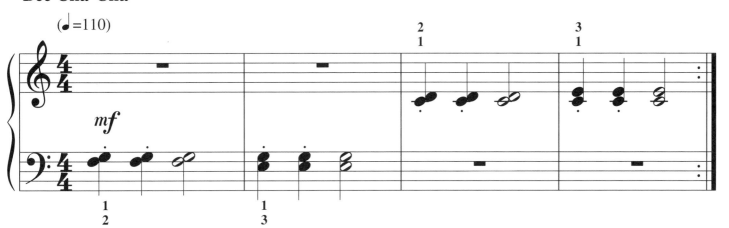

Red Light, Green Light

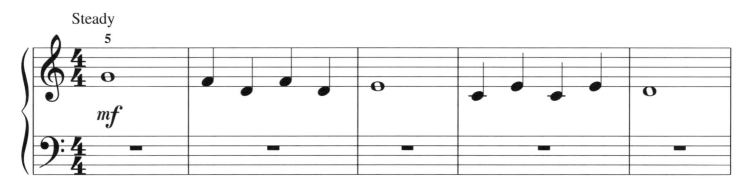

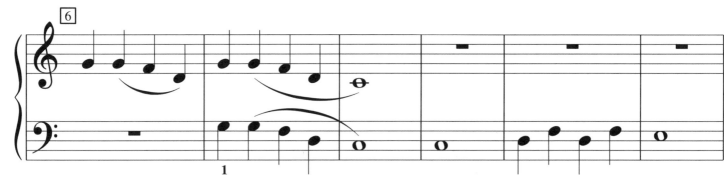

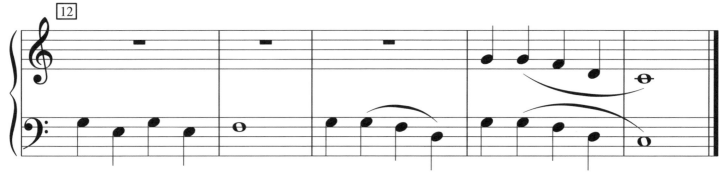

Accompaniment (Student plays two octaves higher than written.) 🔘 **11/12** 💾 **8**

Bee Cha-Cha

Bouncy

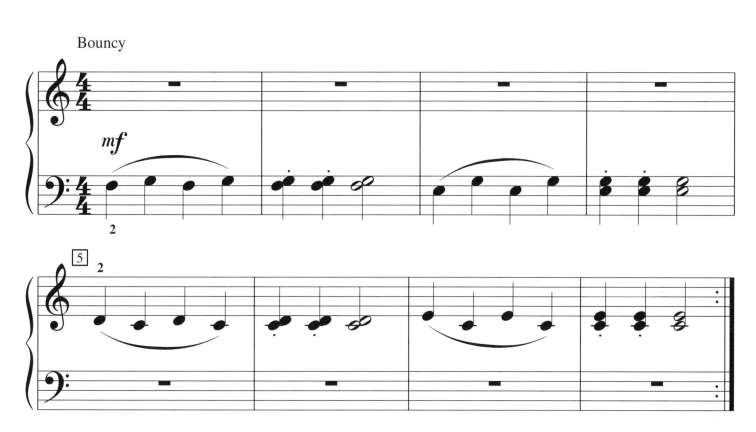

Accompaniment (Student plays two octaves higher than written.)

Bouncy (♩=130)

13

Use with Lesson Book 2, pgs. 10-11

Musical Fitness Plan

Use this checklist to review fitness skills and to focus on learning new ones.

☐ **Hand Position**

☐ **Beautiful Tone**

☐ **Attention to Silence**

☐ **Playing** *Piano*

☐ **Connected Tones –** *Legato*

☐ **Detached Tones –** *Staccato*

To the Teacher: Demonstrate these warm-ups first. This will allow students to focus on the purely physical aspects of learning a new skill. Encourage students to play each warm-up in different octaves.

Warm-Ups

Tiptoe *pg. 16*

 15

Pretend you are sneaking up on your friends. Step quietly so they won't hear you! As you tiptoe along, take smaller steps (2nds) and larger steps (4ths).

Feel the difference in your fingers between the 2nds and 4ths. Think ahead!

Play quietly! Let go of each key as soon as you play it, letting your wrist bounce lightly. Notice how your fingers naturally rebound and come to rest on the keys.

Windchimes *pg. 17*

 16

Imagine windchimes circling in the wind. Imitate their round, ringing sound and their swirling motion.

Pass the sound smoothly from one finger to the next. Begin each phrase with a downward motion of the arm and end the phrase with an upward motion of the wrist.

Tiptoe

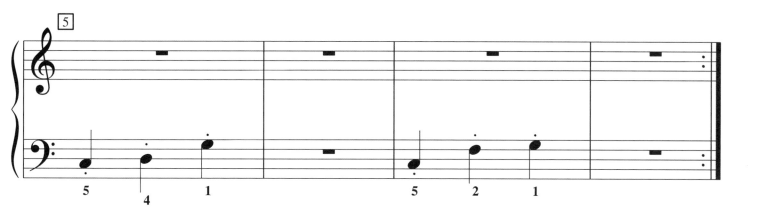

Windchimes

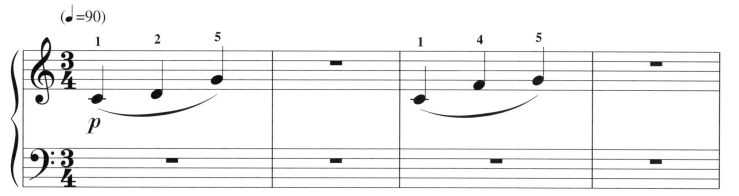

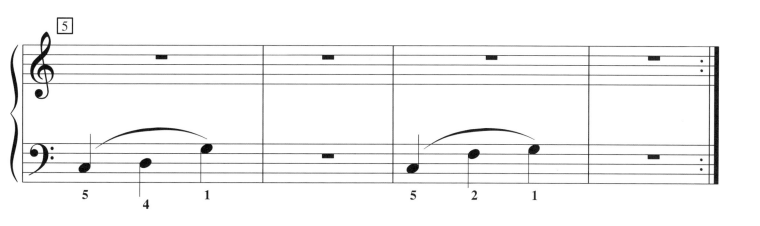

Tiptoe

Cautiously

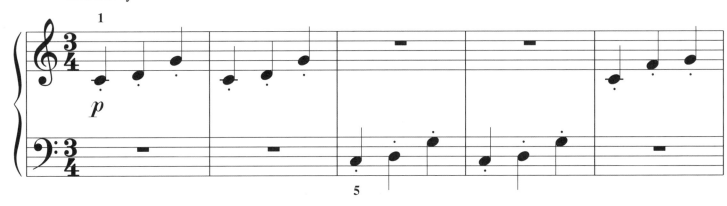

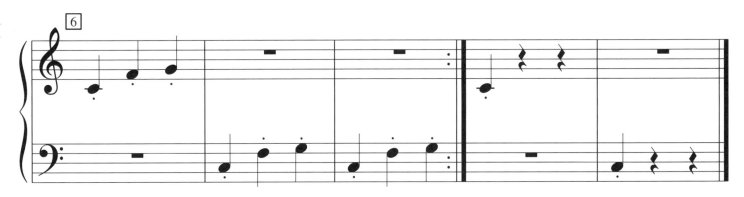

Accompaniment (Student plays one octave lower than written.) 🔘 **17/18** 💾 **12**

Cautiously (♩=120)

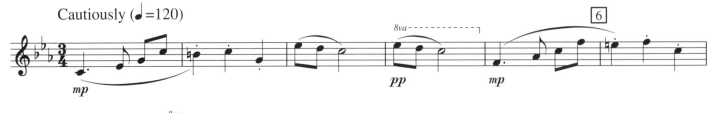

Windchimes

Accompaniment (Student plays two octaves higher than written.)

Use with Lesson Book 2, pg. 13

Musical Fitness Plan

Use this checklist to review fitness skills and to focus on learning new ones.

☐ **Hand Position**

☐ **Beautiful Tone**

☐ **Attention to Silence**

☐ **Playing** *Forte*

☐ **Playing** *Mezzo Forte*

☐ **Playing** *Piano*

NEW!

Playing *Crescendo – Decrescendo*

Gradually change the sound from soft to loud or loud to soft by pressing the key to the bottom of the key bed with increasing or decreasing arm weight. Listen to the sound you create.

☐ **Connected Tones –** *Legato*

☐ **Detached Tones –** *Staccato*

NEW!

Playing Hands Together
When playing hands together with different fingers in each hand, first practice the finger combinations by tapping them away from the piano.

Warm-Ups

Out To Sea *pgs. 20-21*

21

Notes that come before the first full measure are called *upbeats*.

When you play an upbeat, imitate the movement of a wave by gently rolling your hand toward the downbeat. Let your wrist and arm follow.

Mirage *pg. 22*

22

When you speak a sentence, your voice rises and falls with each phrase.

Say the following sentences. Listen to the natural rise and fall of your voice.

Is it desert sand?   **It's a caravan.**

Match this rise and fall as you play the first phrase with a *crescendo* and the second phrase with a *decrescendo*.

Prancing *pg. 23*

23

A prancing horse lifts each leg with a spring in its step.

Let your wrist bounce lightly as you play each *staccato* note. Notice how your fingers rebound naturally and come to rest on the keys.

18

Out To Sea

($\quad$=130)

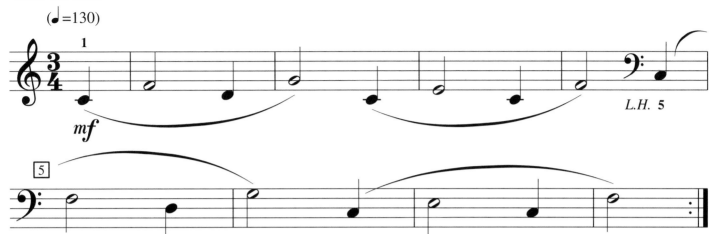

Mirage

($\quad$=95)

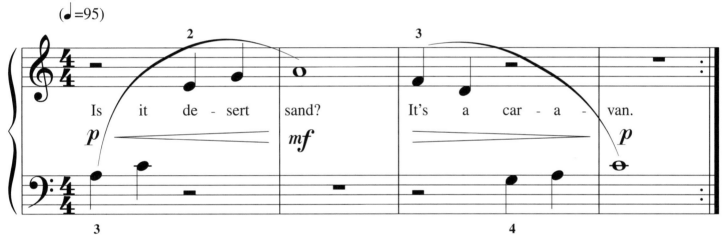

Is it de - sert sand? It's a car - a - van.

Prancing

($\quad$=125)

19

Out To Sea

Smooth sailing

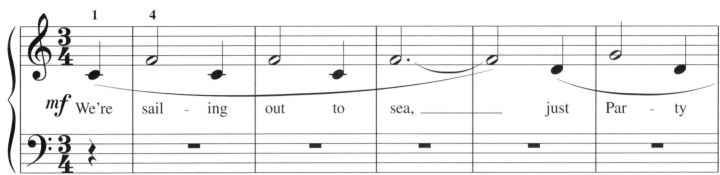

mf We're sail - ing out to sea, _____ just Par - ty

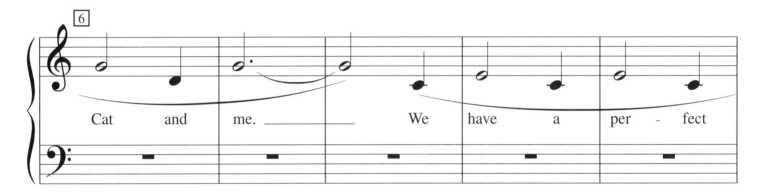

Cat and me. _____ We have a per - fect

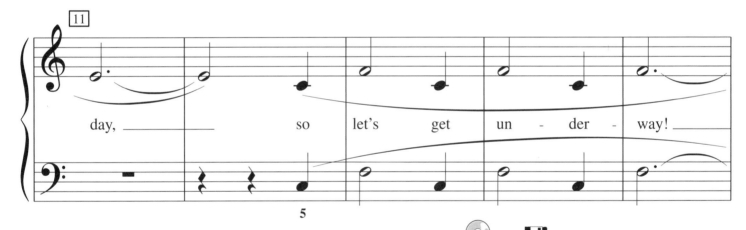

day, _____ so let's get un - der - way!

Accompaniment (Student plays two octaves higher than written.)

Smooth sailing (♩=150)

Lyrics (vocal line):

16 We're sail - ing out to sea, _____ just

21 Par - ty Cat and me. _____ But he for - got the

27 boat, _____ I'm glad that we can float! _____

Mirage

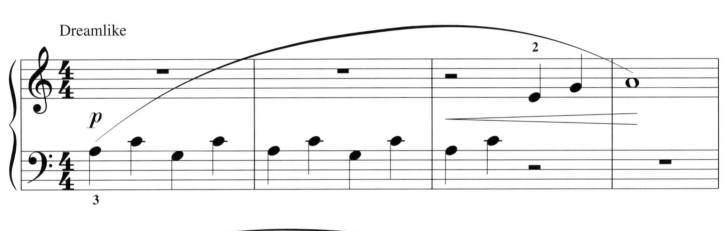

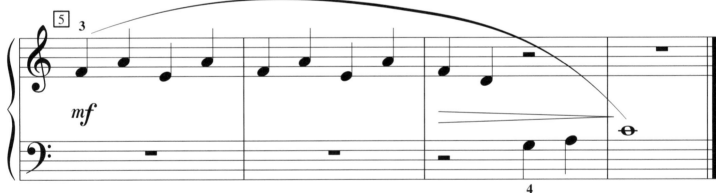

Accompaniment (Student plays one octave higher than written.)

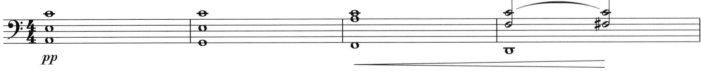

Prancing

Accompaniment (Student plays two octaves higher than written.)

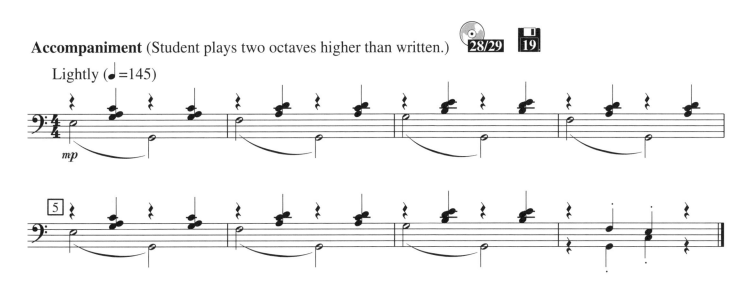

Use with Lesson Book 2, pg. 20

Musical Fitness Plan

Use this checklist to review fitness skills and to focus on learning new ones.

- ☐ **Hand Position**

- ☐ **Beautiful Tone**

- ☐ **Attention to Silence**

- ☐ **Playing *Mezzo Forte***

- ☐ **Playing *Crescendo – Decrescendo***

- ☐ **Connected Tones – *Legato***
  When playing two-note phrases (slurs), use a *drop/lift* motion of the wrist.

- ☐ **Detached Tones – *Staccato***

NEW!

Playing Hands Together
When one hand holds a note and the other plays *staccato*, the coordination requires two different motions at the same time.

To the Teacher: Demonstrate these warm-ups first. This will allow students to focus on the purely physical aspects of learning a new skill. Encourage students to play each warm-up in different octaves.

Warm-Ups

Can You...? *pg. 26*

You Can! *pg. 27*

Many sports activities require two separate motions at the same time. For example, you dribble a basketball while running down the court; you do the crawl stroke while kicking your legs. Can you think of others?

When one hand holds a note while the other hand plays *staccato*, the coordination feels similar to rubbing your stomach while patting your head.

First practice this combination of motions (holding a note in one hand while the other plays *staccato*), by tapping them on the piano fallboard. As you play, listen for the contrast between the long, *legato* sounds and the short, *staccato* sounds.

Outside-In *pg. 28*

Inside-Out *pg. 29*

When you drop a basketball, you release it with a downward motion of your arm. When it rebounds it causes an upward motion of your wrist.

When playing a two-note phrase (slur), use a similar *drop/lift* motion.

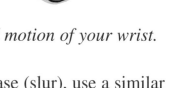

Downward motion of the arm — Upward motion of the wrist

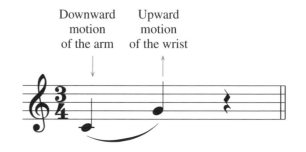

Can You...?

(♩=120)

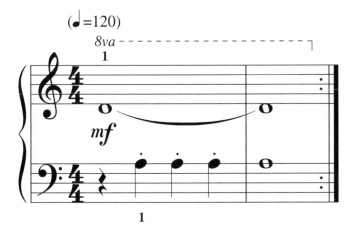

You Can!

(♩=120)

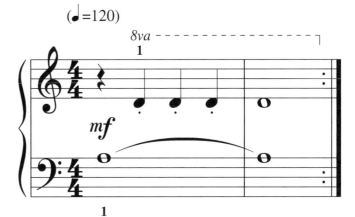

Repeat, using   R.H. 2 - L.H. 2   R.H. 4 - L.H. 4
                        R.H. 3 - L.H. 3   R.H. 5 - L.H. 5

Outside-In

(♩=130)

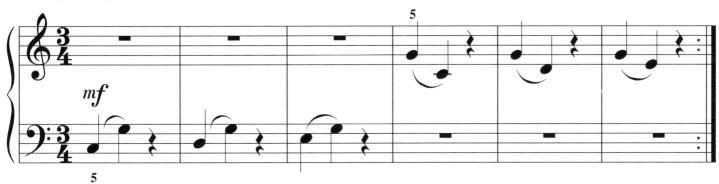

Inside-Out

(♩=130)

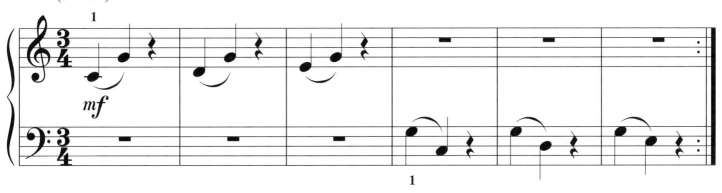

Can You...?

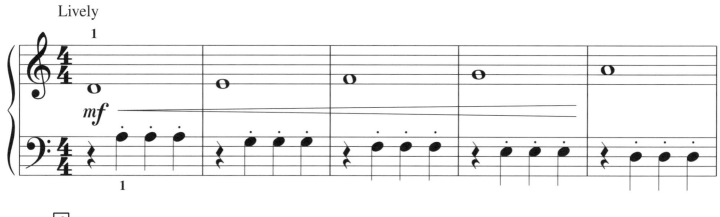

Accompaniment (Student plays one octave higher than written.)

Lively (♩=145)

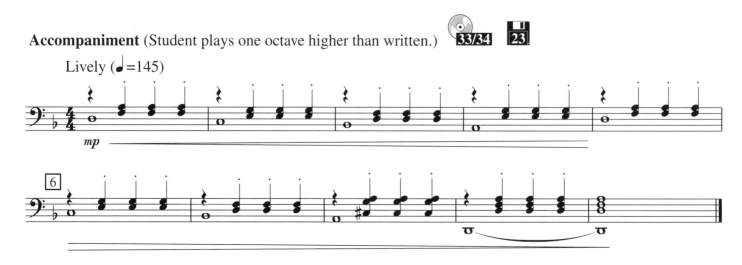

You Can!

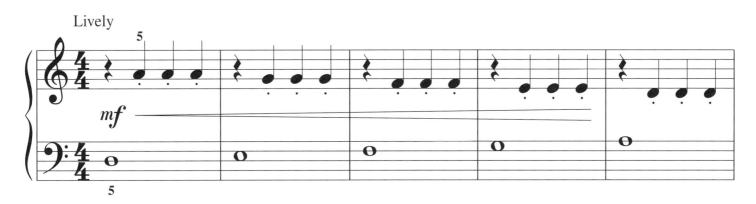

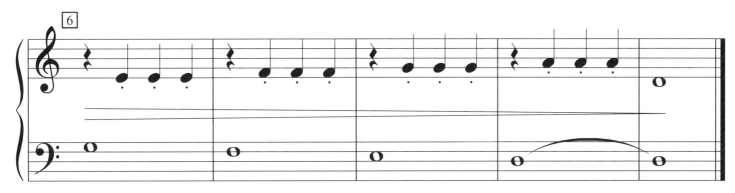

Accompaniment (Student plays one octave higher than written.)

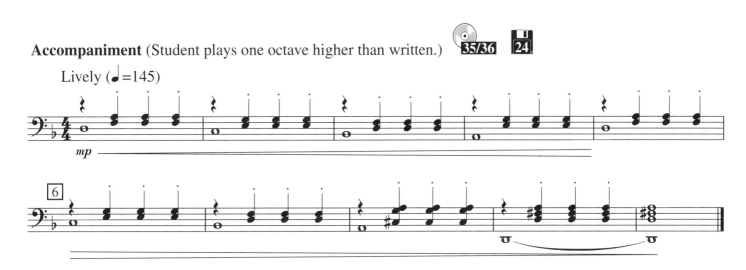

27

Use with Lesson Book 2, pg. 23

Outside-In

Moving along

Accompaniment (Student plays one octave higher than written.) 37/38 25

Moving along (♩=150)

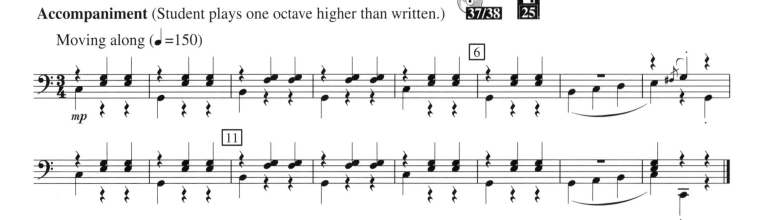

Inside-Out

Accompaniment (Student plays one octave higher than written.)

Moving along (♩=150)

Use with Lesson Book 2, pg. 23

Musical Fitness Plan

Use this checklist to review fitness skills and to focus on learning new ones.

☐ **Hand Position**

☐ **Beautiful Tone**

☐ **Attention to Silence**

Playing *Fortissimo*
Press each key to the bottom of the key bed using maximum arm weight.

☐ **Playing** *Forte*

☐ **Playing** *Piano*

☐ **Connected Tones – *Legato***

☐ **Detached Tones – *Staccato***

☐ **Playing Hands Together**
  • Parallel motion
  • Contrary motion
  • Different fingers in each hand

Warm-Ups

Handbells *pg. 32*

When four hand-bell ringers play together, they must swing their bells at exactly the same moment with the same strength.

When you play several notes at once, drop your weight equally into each key so all the notes sound at exactly the same time. Press each key to the bottom of the key bed, using full arm weight for *f* and less arm weight for *p*.

A-Rest *pg. 33*

While running the ball down the field, a soccer player looks ahead to plan the next move.

When playing different fingers in each hand, think ahead to the next finger combinations.

Handbells

($\quad$=100)

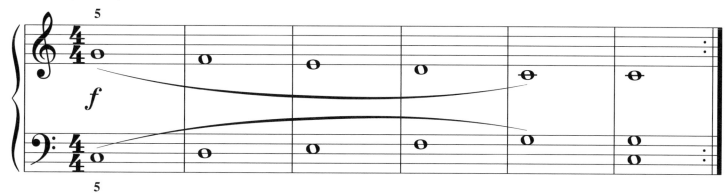

A-Rest

($\quad$=130)

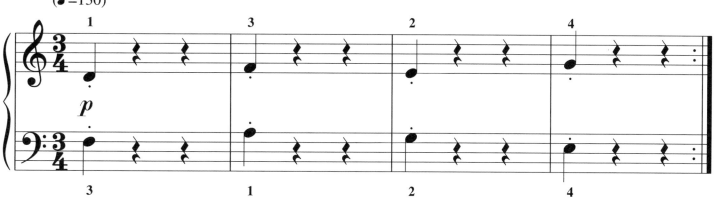

Handbells

Ringing

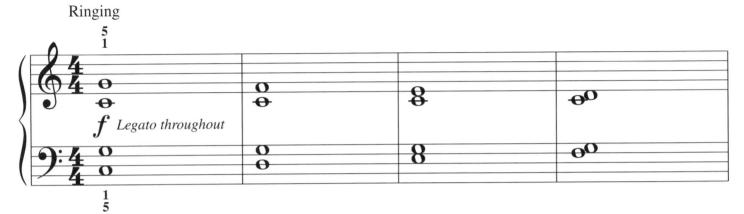

f Legato throughout

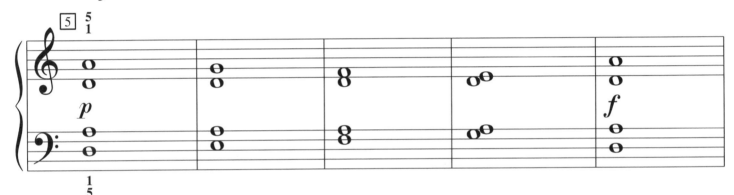

p

f

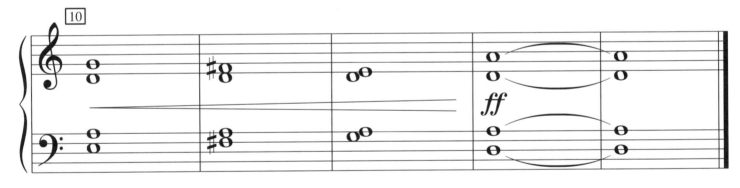

ff

Accompaniment

Ringing (♩=110)   **43/44**   **29**

Play both hands 8va throughout

f Legato throughout with pedal

p

f

ff

Use with Lesson Book 2, pgs. 25-29

A-Rest

Accompaniment (Student plays one octave higher than written.)

Sneaky (♩=150)

Use with Lesson Book 2, pg. 29

Musical Fitness Plan

Use this checklist to review fitness skills and to focus on learning new ones.

- ☐ **Hand Position**
- ☐ **Beautiful Tone**
- ☐ **Attention to Silence**
- ☐ **Playing** *Forte*
- ☐ **Playing** *Mezzo Forte*
- ☐ **Playing** *Piano*
- ☐ **Playing** *Crescendo – Decrescendo*
- ☐ **Connected Tones –** *Legato*

NEW!

Accents
Drop full arm weight into the key to emphasize a single note.

- ☐ **Playing Hands Together**
  - Parallel motion
  - Contrary motion
  - Different fingers in each hand
  - *NEW!* Oblique motion – holding a note in one hand while moving in the other.

NEW!

Playing Black and White Keys Together
When moving from a white key to a black key, move your hand slightly forward for comfort.

Warm-Ups

Meditation *pg. 36*

 47 | 31

In **Meditation**, the right and left hands move hands together in different directions at the same time.

- **Parallel motion** (same)
- **Contrary motion** (opposite)
- **Oblique motion** (holding/moving)

Before playing this warm-up, practice these motions away from the piano, using large arm movements.

As you play this warm-up, use the same arm movements you practiced away from the piano. Let your arms follow your fingers in **parallel** or **contrary** motions.

Too Cool! *pg. 37*

 48 | 32

Have you ever noticed how "cool" you feel when you're wearing your sunglasses and a favorite hat?

Notice the way certain combinations of black and white keys sound "cool."

Meditation

($\quad$=85)

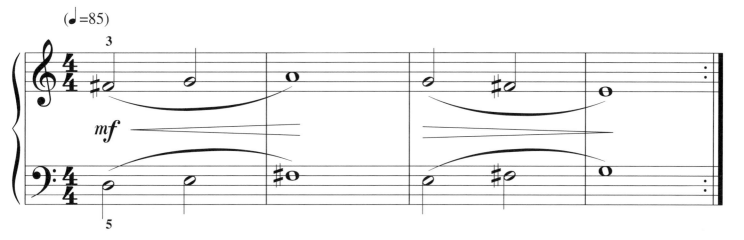

Too Cool!

($\quad$=80)

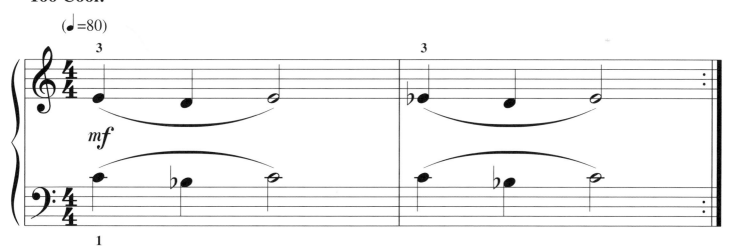

Meditation

Peacefully

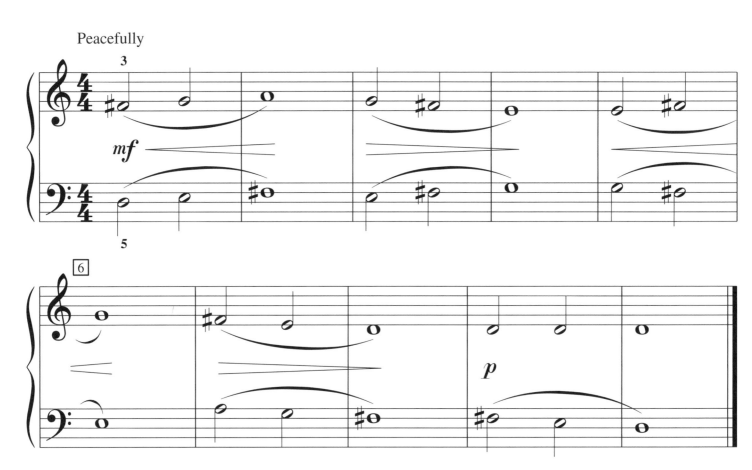

Accompaniment (Student plays one octave higher than written.)

Peacefully (♩=95)

Too Cool!

Slow Blues

Accompaniment (Student plays one octave higher than written.) [51/52] [34]

Slow Blues (♫ = ♩ ♪)(♩=100)

Use with Lesson Book 2, pgs. 32-39

Musical Fitness Plan

In these etudes you will combine many of the technical skills you have learned in *Piano Technique Book 2*.

☐ **Hand Position**

☐ **Beautiful Tone**

☐ **Attention to Silence**

☐ **Playing *Mezzo Forte***

☐ **Playing *Piano***

NEW!

Playing *Pianissimo*
Press each key to the bottom of the key bed using minimum arm weight.

☐ **Connected Tones – *Legato***

☐ **Detached Tones – *Staccato***

☐ **Playing Hands Together**
- Parallel motion
- Contrary motion
- Oblique motion
- Different fingers in each hand
- Holding a note in one hand and playing *legato* in the other

Warm-Ups

Meet In The Middle *pg. 39*

Imagine that you and a friend are playing on a rope bridge. Beginning at opposite ends of the bridge, you both move steadily towards each other to meet in the middle. Then you both turn and move to the opposite ends again.

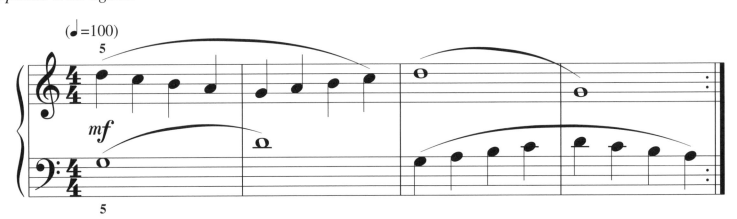

Scattered Showers *pg. 40*

A steady, spring shower falls evenly and lightly from the sky. When the shower is nearly over, small droplets continue to fall.

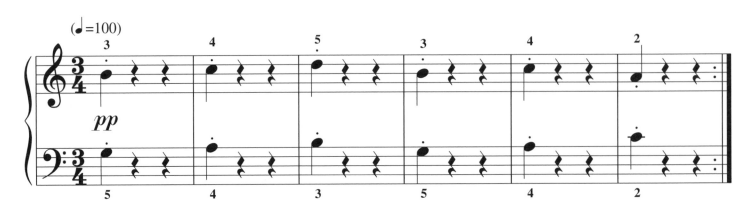

Meet In The Middle

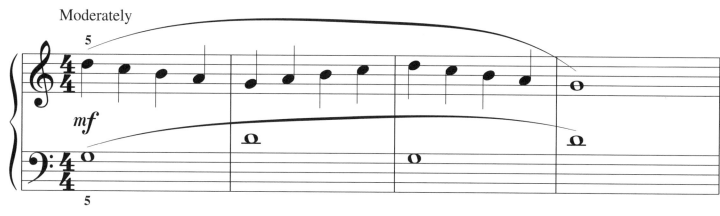

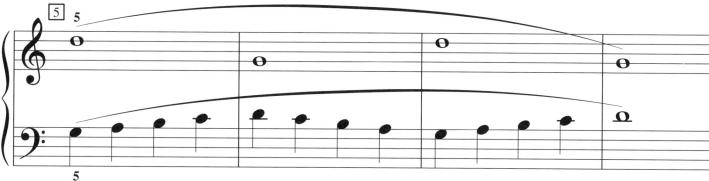

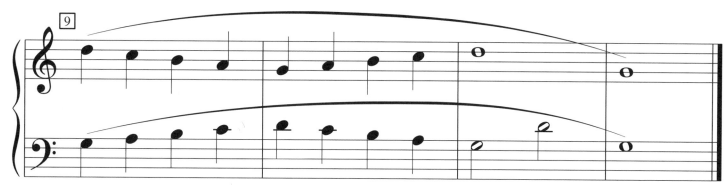

Accompaniment (Student plays one octave higher than written.)

Use with Lesson Book 2, pgs. 40-43

Scattered Showers

Accompaniment

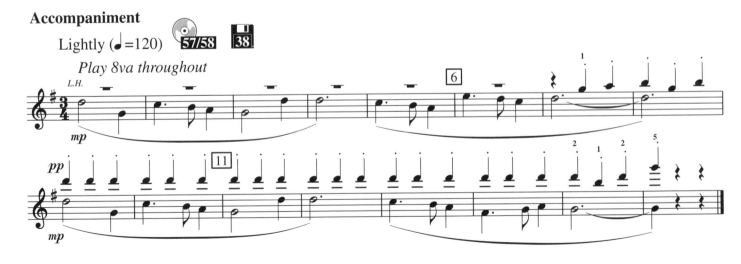

Use with Lesson Book 2, pgs. 45-47